# THE MIRACLE ON ICE

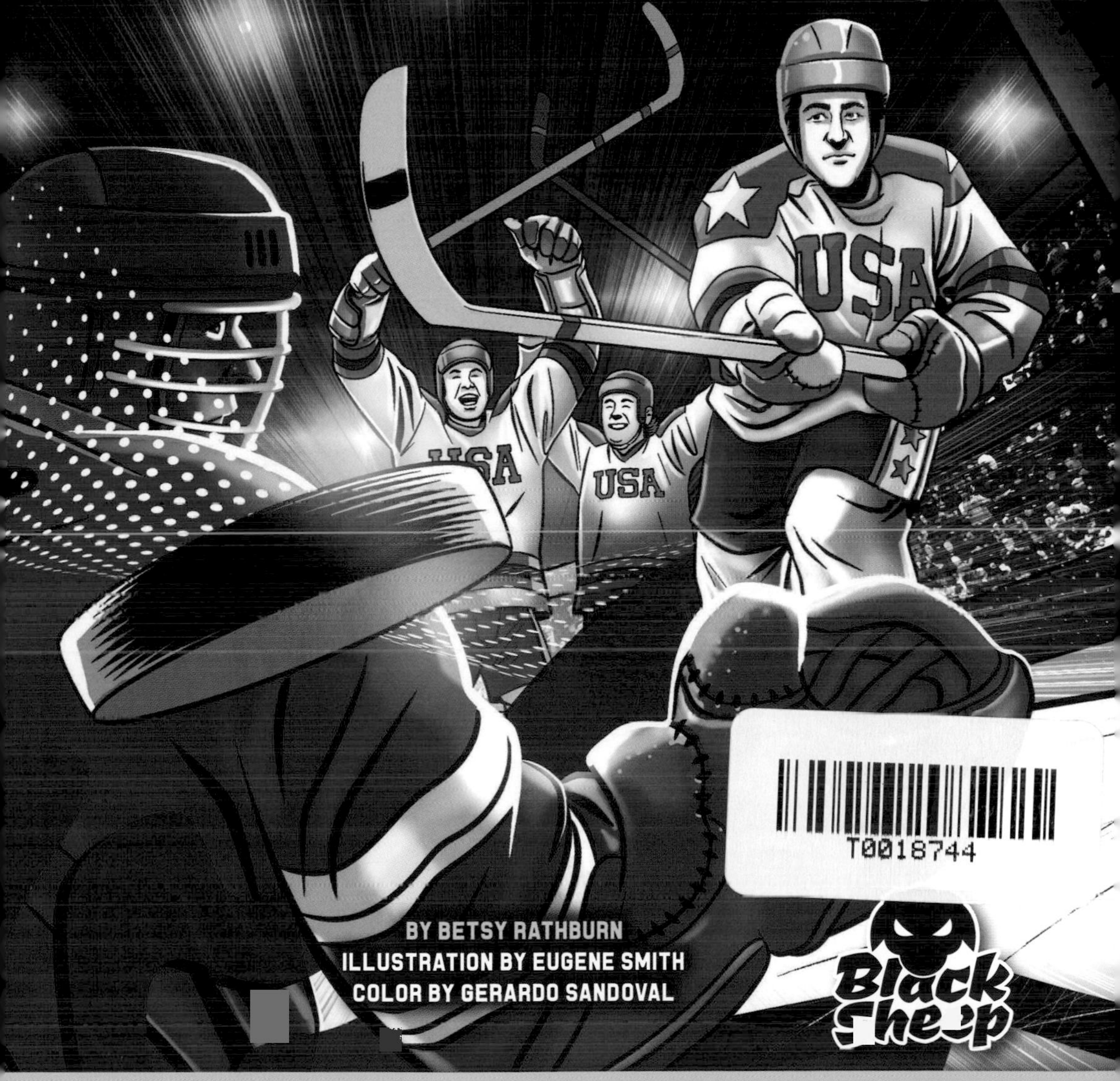
USA
USA
USA



BY BETSY RATHBURN
ILLUSTRATION BY EUGENE SMITH
COLOR BY GERARDO SANDOVAL

Black Sheep

BELLWETHER MEDIA • MINNEAPOLIS, MN

STRAY FROM REGULAR READS
WITH BLACK SHEEP BOOKS.
FEEL A RUSH WITH EVERY READ!

This edition first published in 2024 by Bellwether Media, Inc.

No part of this publication may be reproduced in whole or in part without written permission of the publisher.
For information regarding permission, write to Bellwether Media, Inc., Attention: Permissions Department,
6012 Blue Circle Drive, Minnetonka, MN 55343.

Library of Congress Cataloging-in-Publication Data

Names: Rathburn, Betsy, author. | Smith, Eugene (Illustrator), illustrator.
Title: The miracle on ice / by Betsy Rathburn ; [illustrated by Eugene Smith].
Description: Minneapolis, MN : Bellwether Media, Inc., 2024. | Series: Black sheep : Greatest moments in sports | Includes
  bibliographical references and index. | Audience: Ages 7-13 years | Audience: Grades 4-6 | Summary:
  "Exciting illustrations follow the events of the Miracle on Ice hockey game. The combination of brightly colored panels
  and leveled text is intended for students in grades 3 through 8"– Provided by publisher.
Identifiers: LCCN 2023017804 (print) | LCCN 2023017805 (ebook) | ISBN 9798886875089 (library binding) |
  ISBN 9798886875584 (paperback) | ISBN 9798886876963 (ebook)
Subjects: LCSH: Olympic Winter Games (13th : 1980 : Lake Placid, N.Y.)–Juvenile literature. | Hockey players–
  United States–Juvenile literature. | Hockey players–Soviet Union–Juvenile literature. | Hockey–United States–History–
  20th century–Juvenile literature.
Classification: LCC GV848.4.U6 R3 2024 (print) | LCC GV848.4.U6 (ebook) |
  DDC 796.9620973–dc23/eng/20230523
LC record available at https://lccn.loc.gov/2023017804
LC ebook record available at https://lccn.loc.gov/2023017805

Editor: Christina Leaf    Designer: Andrea Schneider

Printed in the United States of America, North Mankato, MN.

# TABLE OF CONTENTS



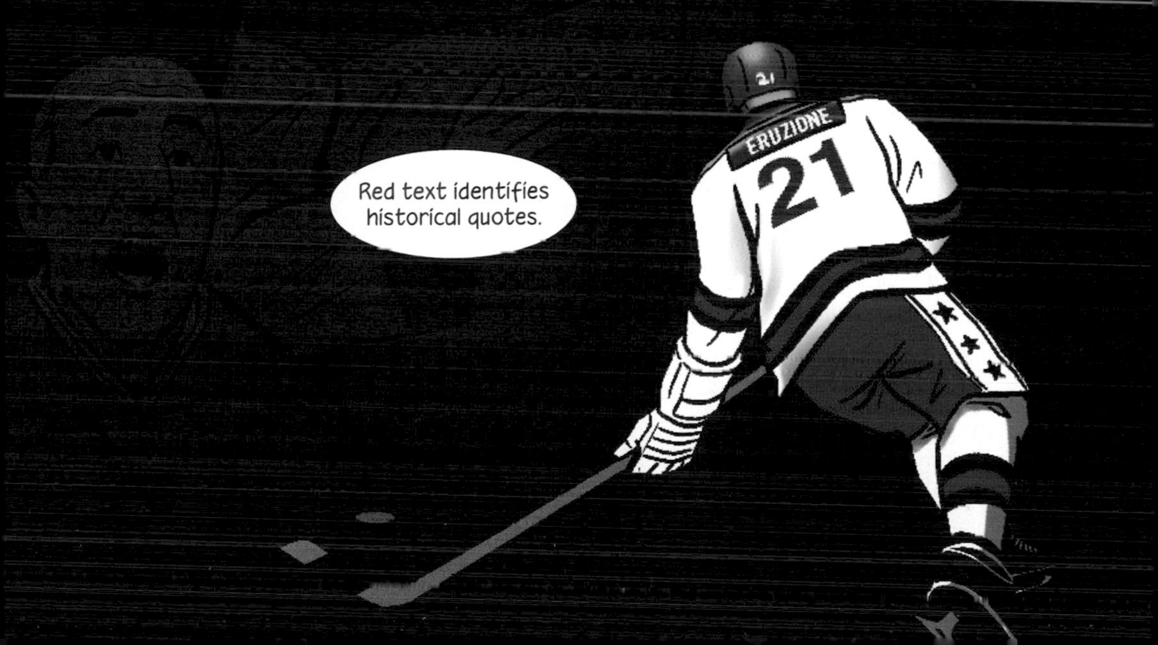
21
ERUZIONE
21
Red text identifies historical quotes.

# BECOMING A TEAM

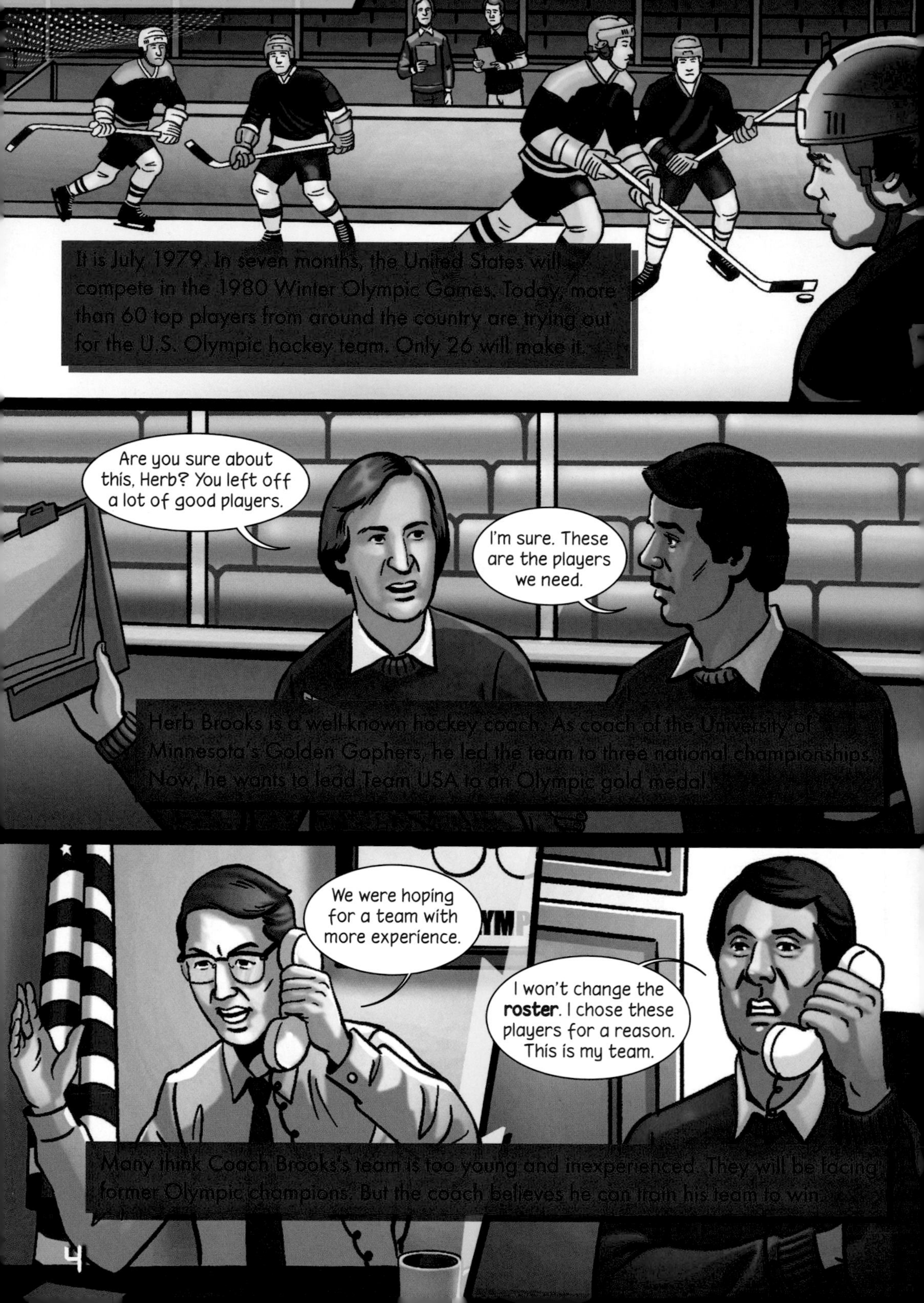

It is July 1979. In seven months, the United States will compete in the 1980 Winter Olympic Games. Today, more than 60 top players from around the country are trying out for the U.S. Olympic hockey team. Only 26 will make it.
Are you sure about this, Herb? You left off a lot of good players.
I'm sure. These are the players we need.
Herb Brooks is a well-known hockey coach. As coach of the University of Minnesota's Golden Gophers, he led the team to three national championships. Now, he wants to lead Team USA to an Olympic gold medal.
We were hoping for a team with more experience.
I won't change the **roster**. I chose these players for a reason. This is my team.
Many think Coach Brooks's team is too young and inexperienced. They will be facing former Olympic champions. But the coach believes he can train his team to win.

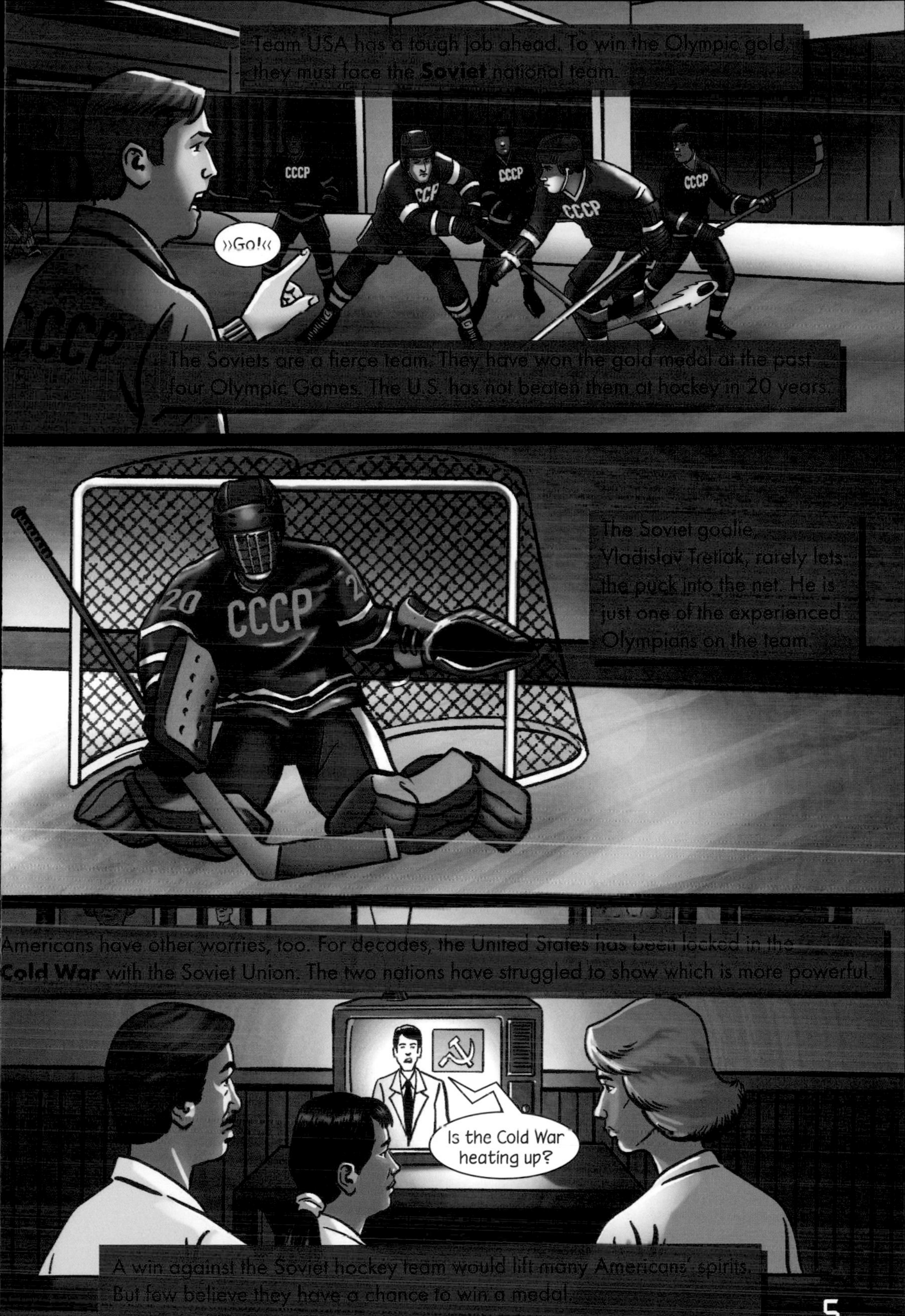
Team USA has a tough job ahead. To win the Olympic gold, they must face the **Soviet** national team.
CCCP
»Go!«
The Soviets are a fierce team. They have won the gold medal at the past four Olympic Games. The U.S. has not beaten them at hockey in 20 years.
CCCP
The Soviet goalie, Vladislav Tretiak, rarely lets the puck into the net. He is just one of the experienced Olympians on the team.
Americans have other worries, too. For decades, the United States has been locked in the **Cold War** with the Soviet Union. The two nations have struggled to show which is more powerful.
Is the Cold War heating up?
A win against the Soviet hockey team would lift many Americans' spirits. But few believe they have a chance to win a medal.

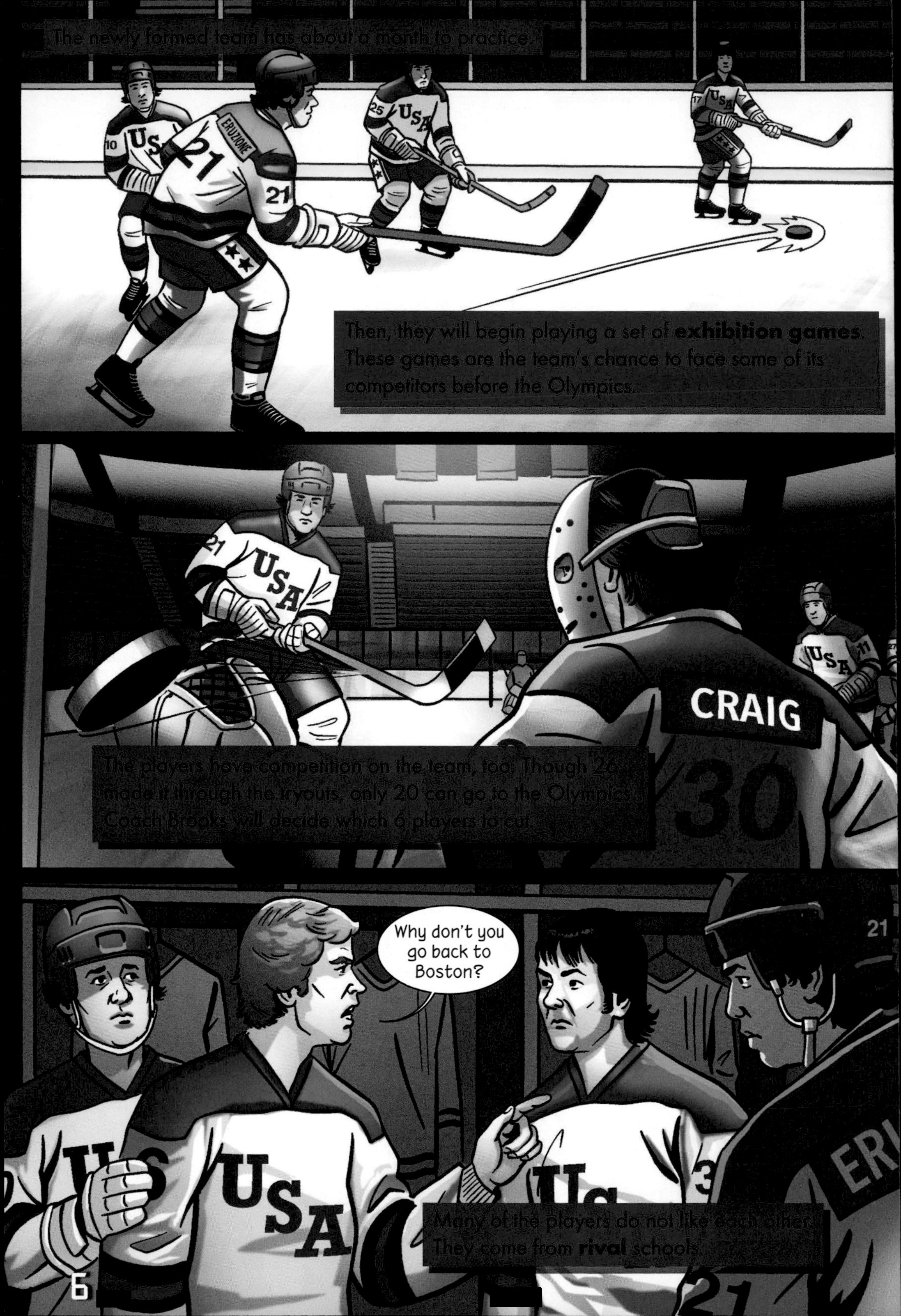
The newly formed team has about a month to practice.
ERUZIONE
Then, they will begin playing a set of **exhibition games**. These games are the team's chance to face some of its competitors before the Olympics.
CRAIG
The players have competition on the team, too. Though 26 made it through the tryouts, only 20 can go to the Olympics. Coach Brooks will decide which 6 players to cut.
Why don't you go back to Boston?
Many of the players do not like each other. They come from **rival** schools.

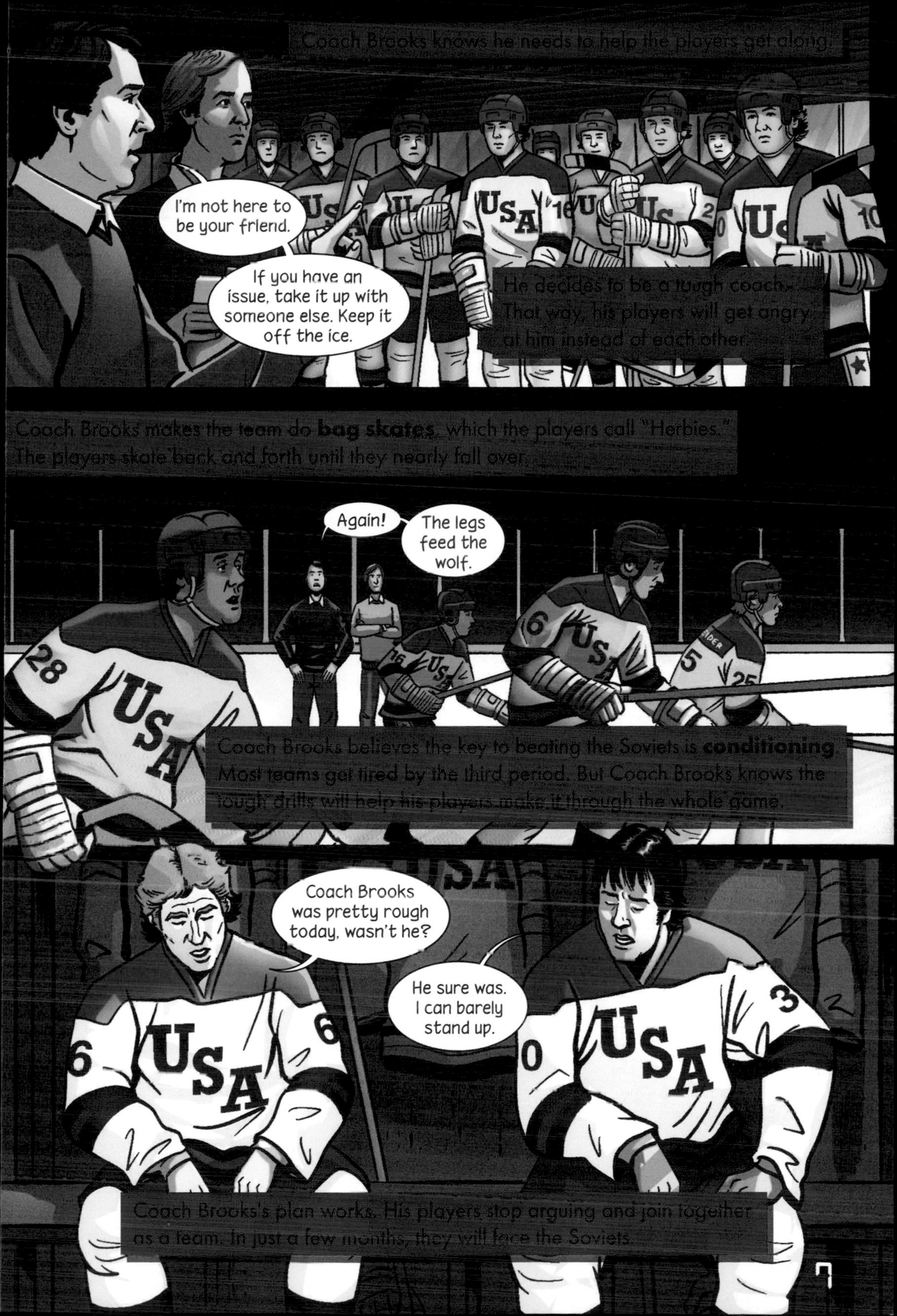
Coach Brooks knows he needs to help the players get along.
I'm not here to be your friend.
If you have an issue, take it up with someone else. Keep it off the ice.
He decides to be a tough coach. That way, his players will get angry at him instead of each other.
Coach Brooks makes the team do **bag skates**, which the players call "Herbies." The players skate back and forth until they nearly fall over.
Again!
The legs feed the wolf.
Coach Brooks believes the key to beating the Soviets is **conditioning**. Most teams get tired by the third period. But Coach Brooks knows the tough drills will help his players make it through the whole game.
Coach Brooks was pretty rough today, wasn't he?
He sure was. I can barely stand up.
Coach Brooks's plan works. His players stop arguing and join together as a team. In just a few months, they will face the Soviets.

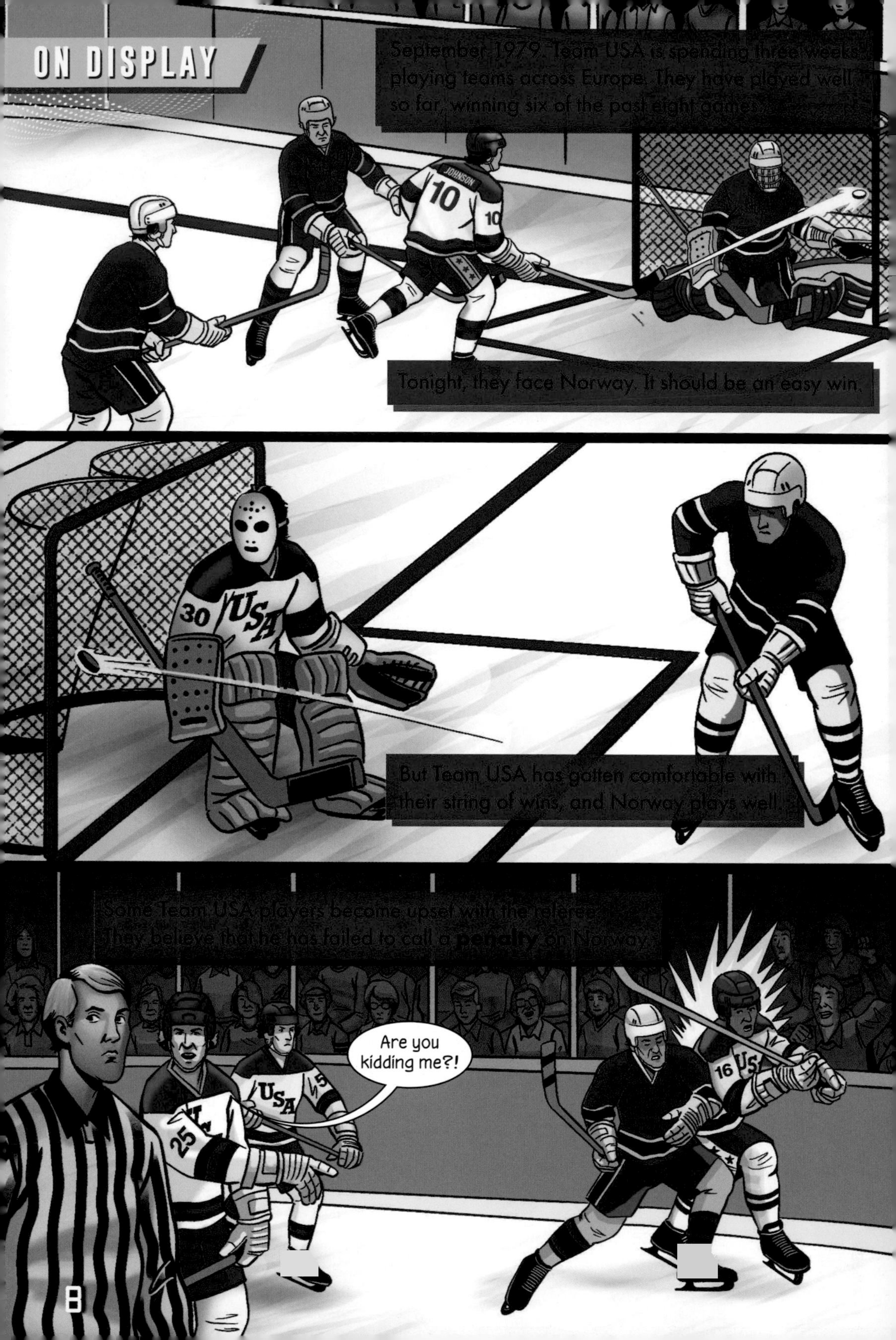
September 1979. Team USA is spending three weeks playing teams across Europe. They have played well so far, winning six of the past eight games.
JOHNSON
10
Tonight, they face Norway. It should be an easy win.
30 USA
But Team USA has gotten comfortable with their string of wins, and Norway plays well.
Some Team USA players become upset with the referee. They believe that he has failed to call a **penalty** on Norway.
Are you kidding me?!
USA
25
16

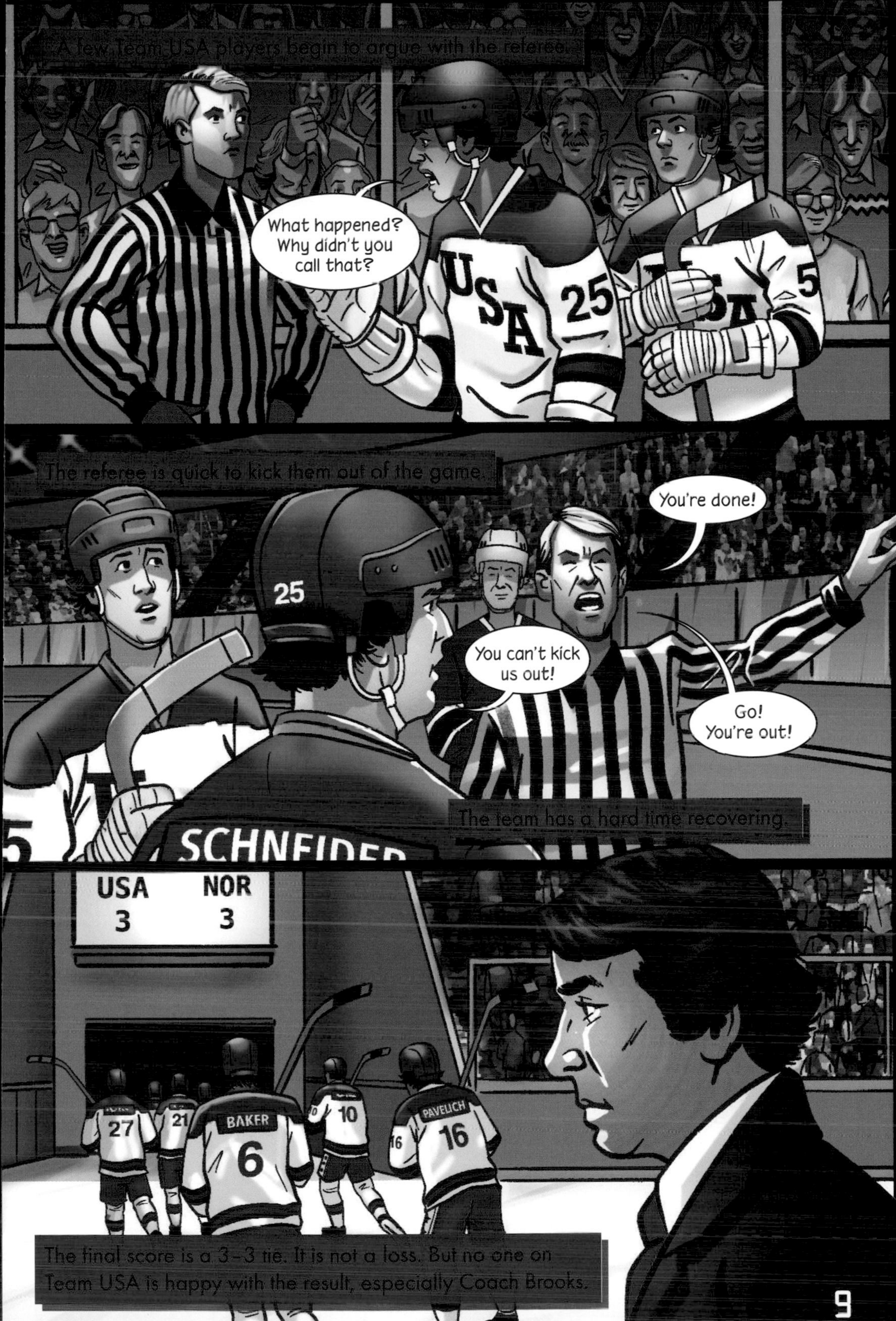
A few Team USA players begin to argue with the referee.
What happened? Why didn't you call that?
USA
25
5
The referee is quick to kick them out of the game.
You're done!
25
You can't kick us out!
Go! You're out!
SCHNEIDER
The team has a hard time recovering.
USA 3
NOR 3
27
21
BAKER
6
10
PAVELICH
16
The final score is a 3–3 tie. It is not a loss. But no one on Team USA is happy with the result, especially Coach Brooks.

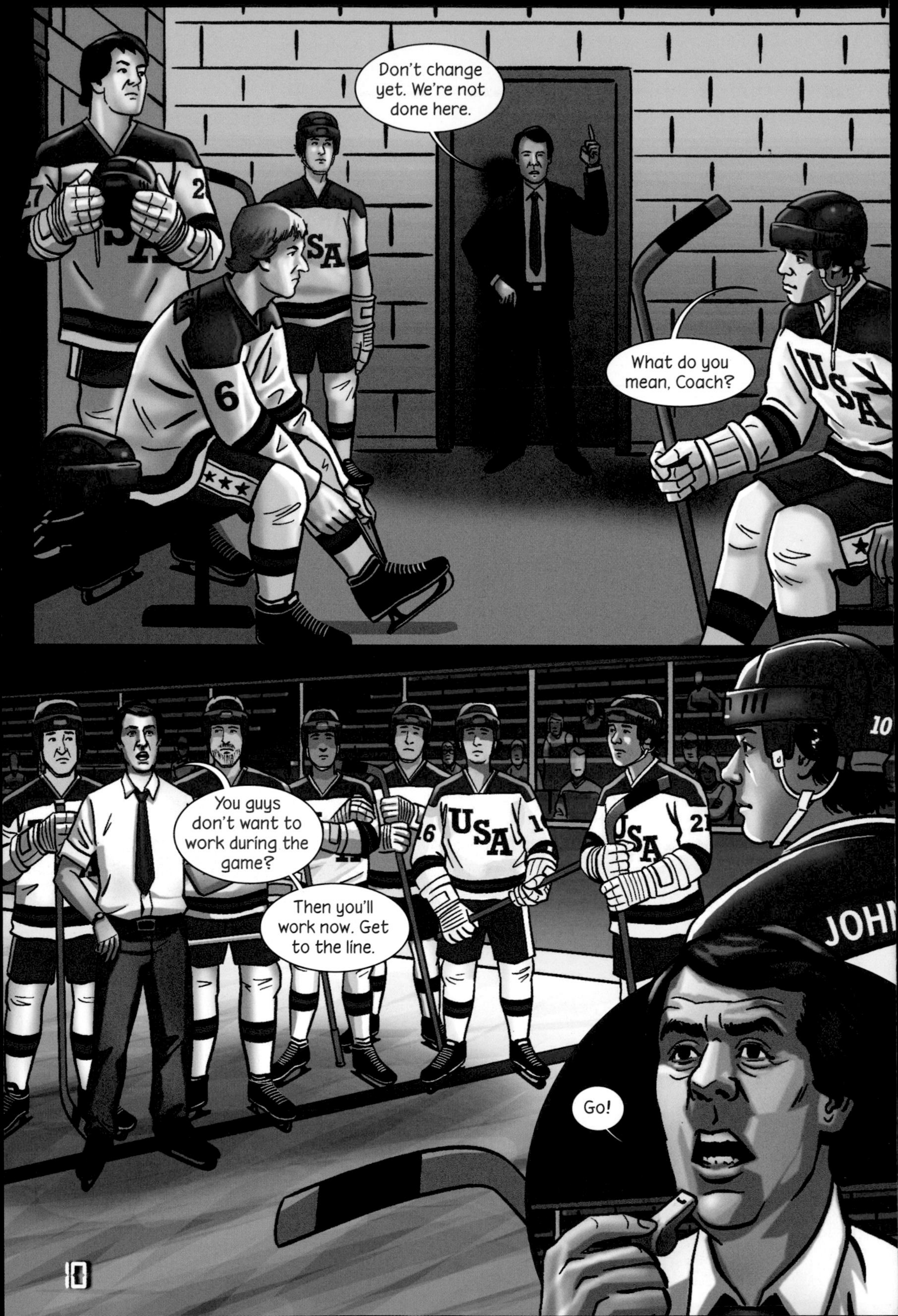
Don't change yet. We're not done here.
What do you mean, Coach?
You guys don't want to work during the game?
Then you'll work now. Get to the line.
Go!

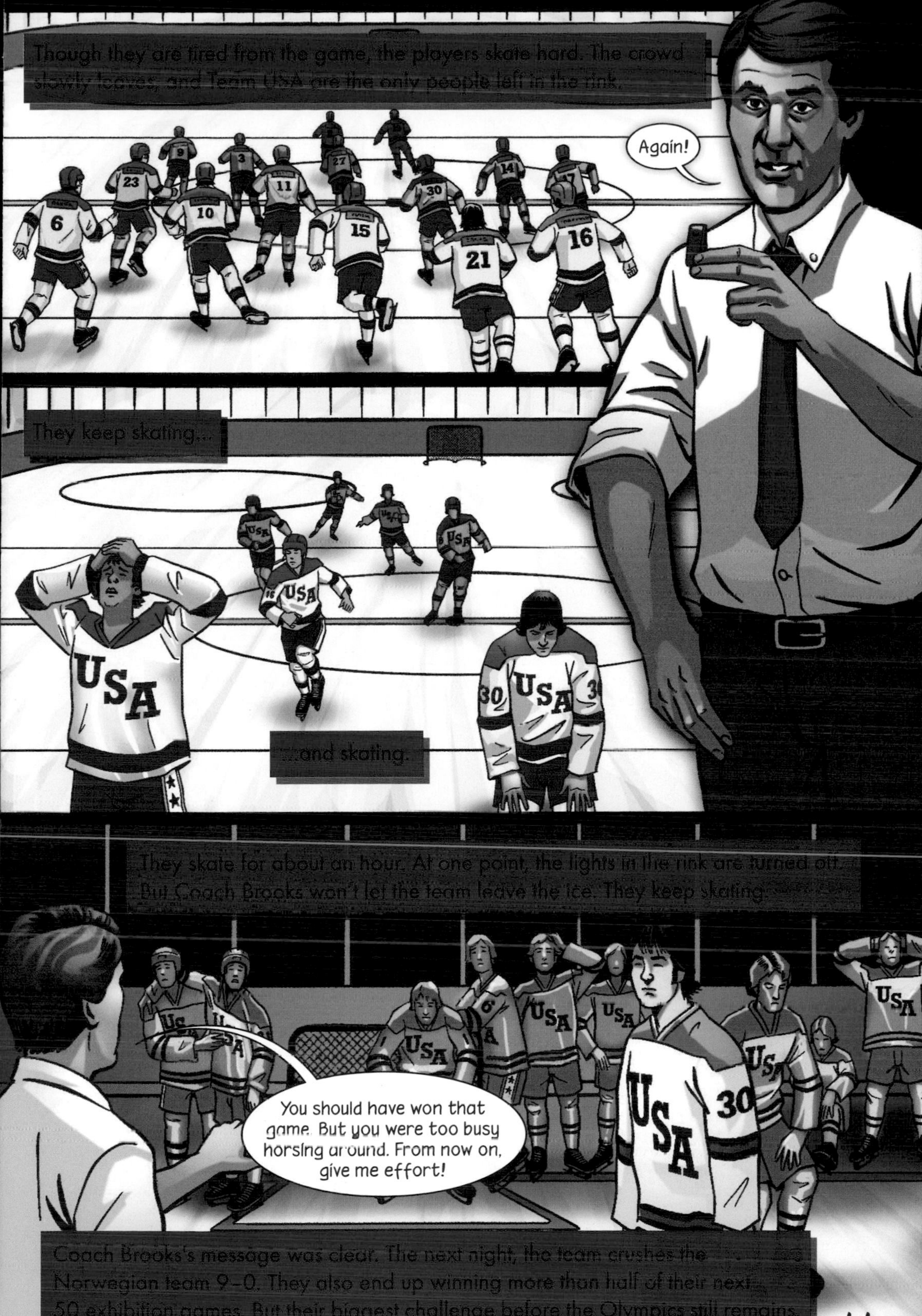
Though they are tired from the game, the players skate hard. The crowd slowly leaves, and Team USA are the only people left in the rink.
Again!
They keep skating...
...and skating.
They skate for about an hour. At one point, the lights in the rink are turned off. But Coach Brooks won't let the team leave the ice. They keep skating.
You should have won that game. But you were too busy horsing around. From now on, give me effort!
Coach Brooks's message was clear. The next night, the team crushes the Norwegian team 9–0. They also end up winning more than half of their next 50 exhibition games. But their biggest challenge before the Olympics still remains.

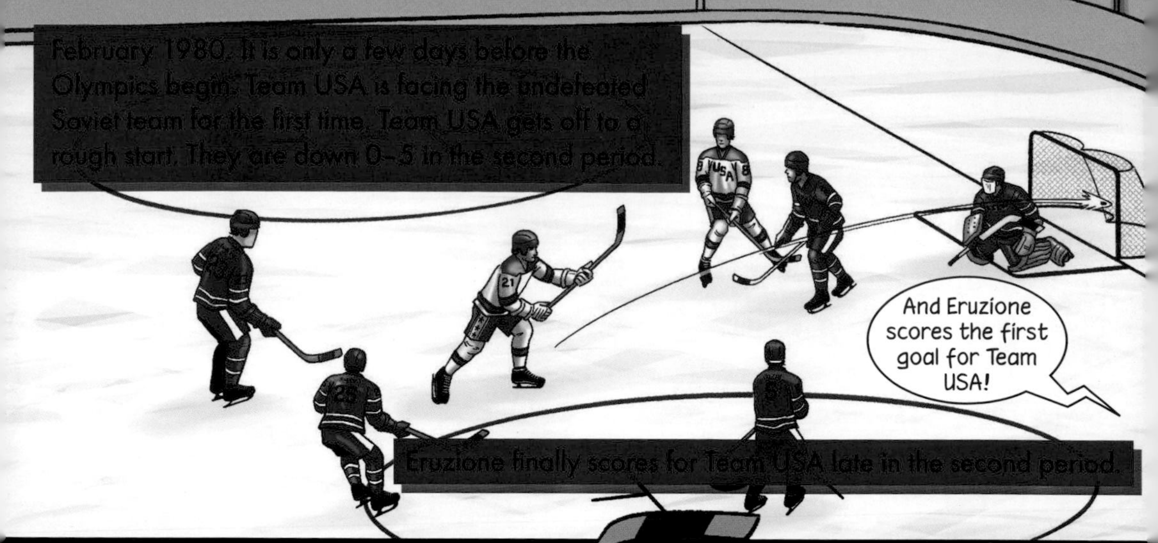
February 1980. It is only a few days before the Olympics begin. Team USA is facing the undefeated Soviet team for the first time. Team USA gets off to a rough start. They are down 0–5 in the second period.
And Eruzione scores the first goal for Team USA!
Eruzione finally scores for Team USA late in the second period.

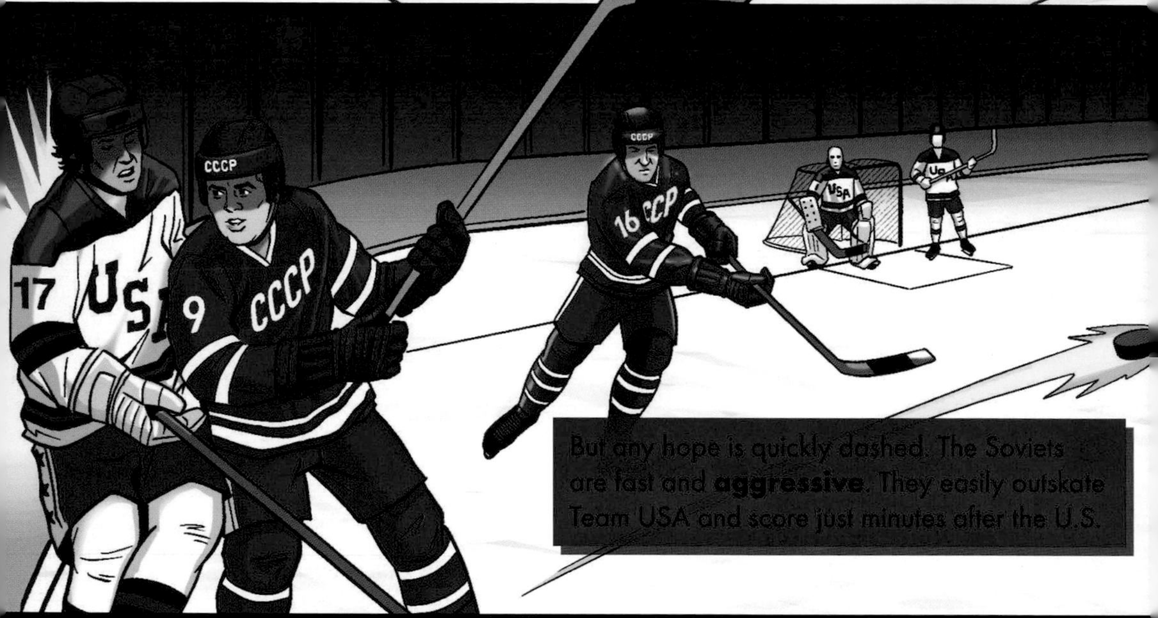
But any hope is quickly dashed. The Soviets are fast and **aggressive**. They easily outskate Team USA and score just minutes after the U.S.

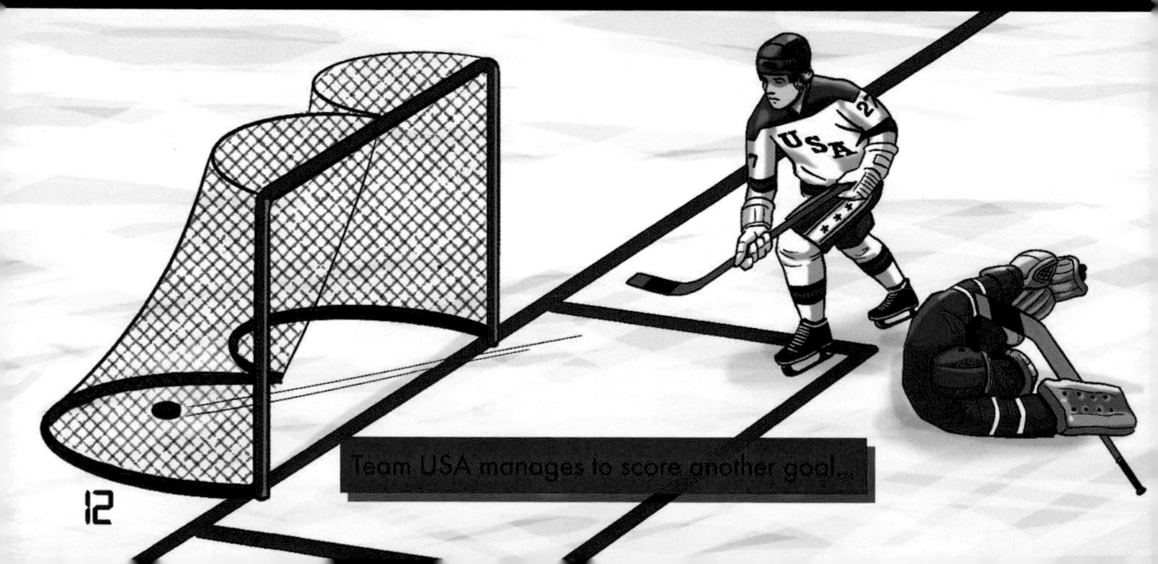
Team USA manages to score another goal...

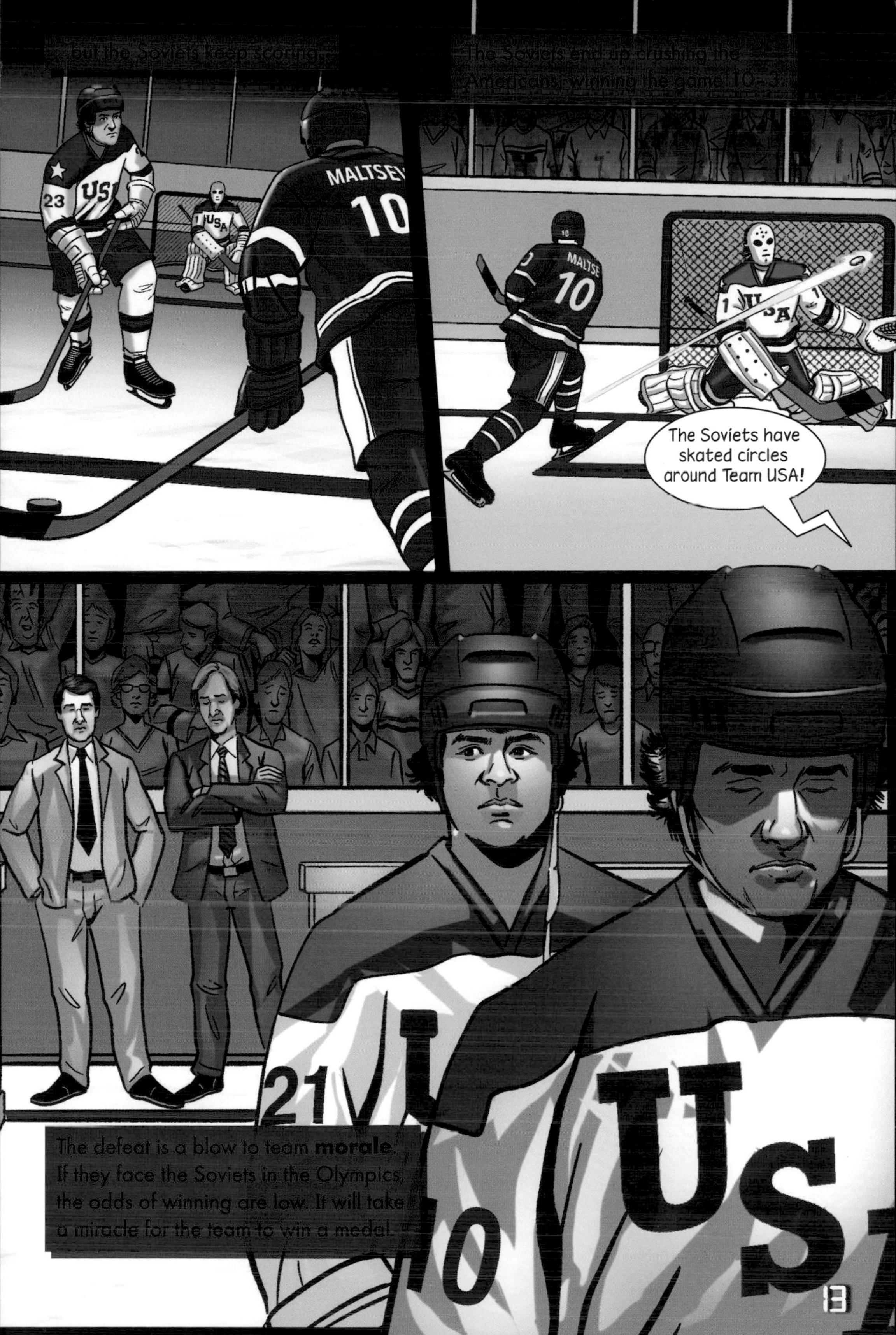
...but the Soviets keep scoring...
The Soviets end up crushing the Americans, winning the game 10–3.
MALTSEV
10
USA
23
The Soviets have skated circles around Team USA!
21
The defeat is a blow to team **morale**. If they face the Soviets in the Olympics, the odds of winning are low. It will take a miracle for the team to win a medal.

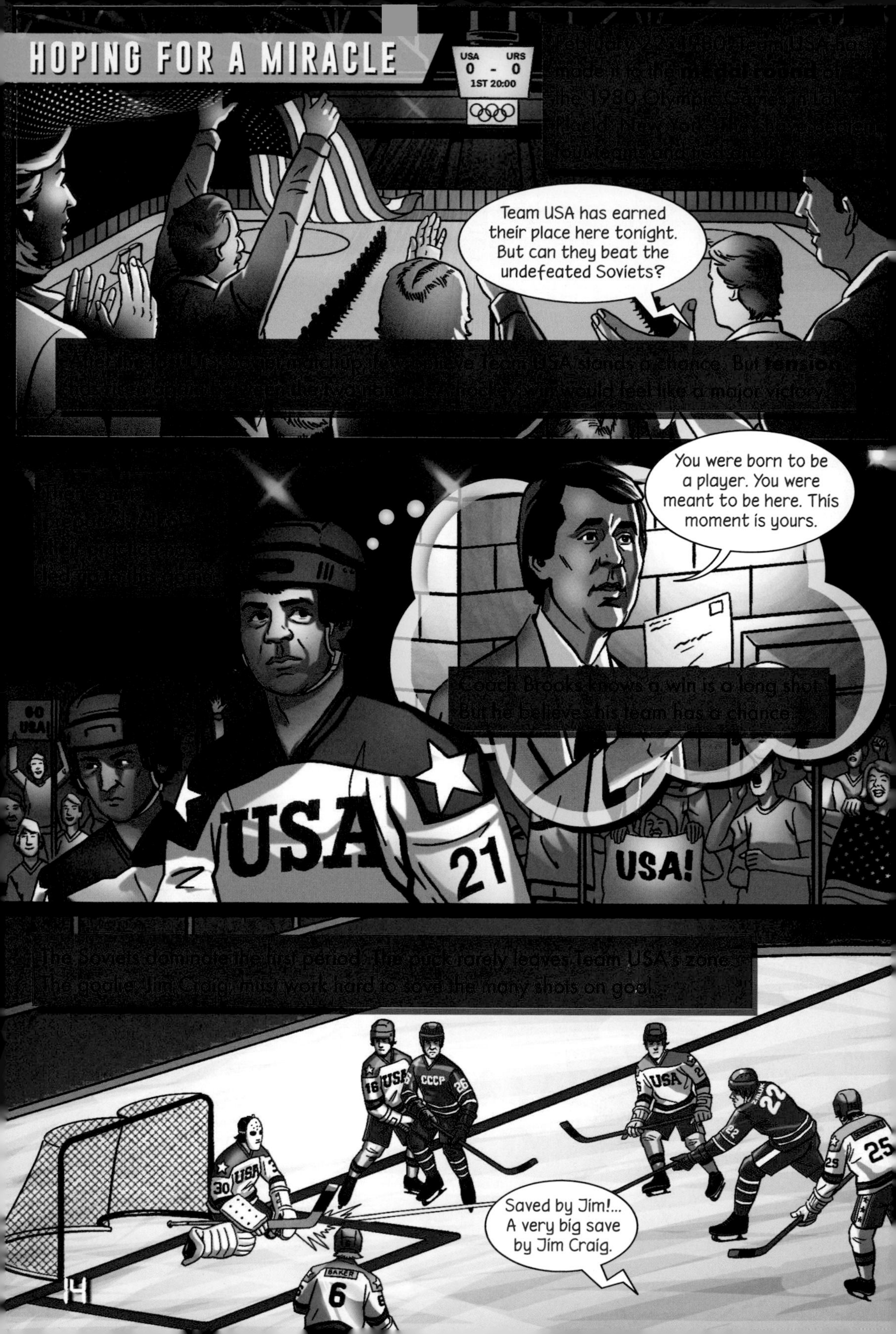
HOPING FOR A MIRACLE
USA URS
0 - 0
1ST 20:00
[redacted]
Team USA has earned their place here tonight. But can they beat the undefeated Soviets?
[redacted]
[redacted]
You were born to be a player. You were meant to be here. This moment is yours.
[redacted]
GO USA!
USA
21
USA!
[redacted]
Saved by Jim!... A very big save by Jim Craig.

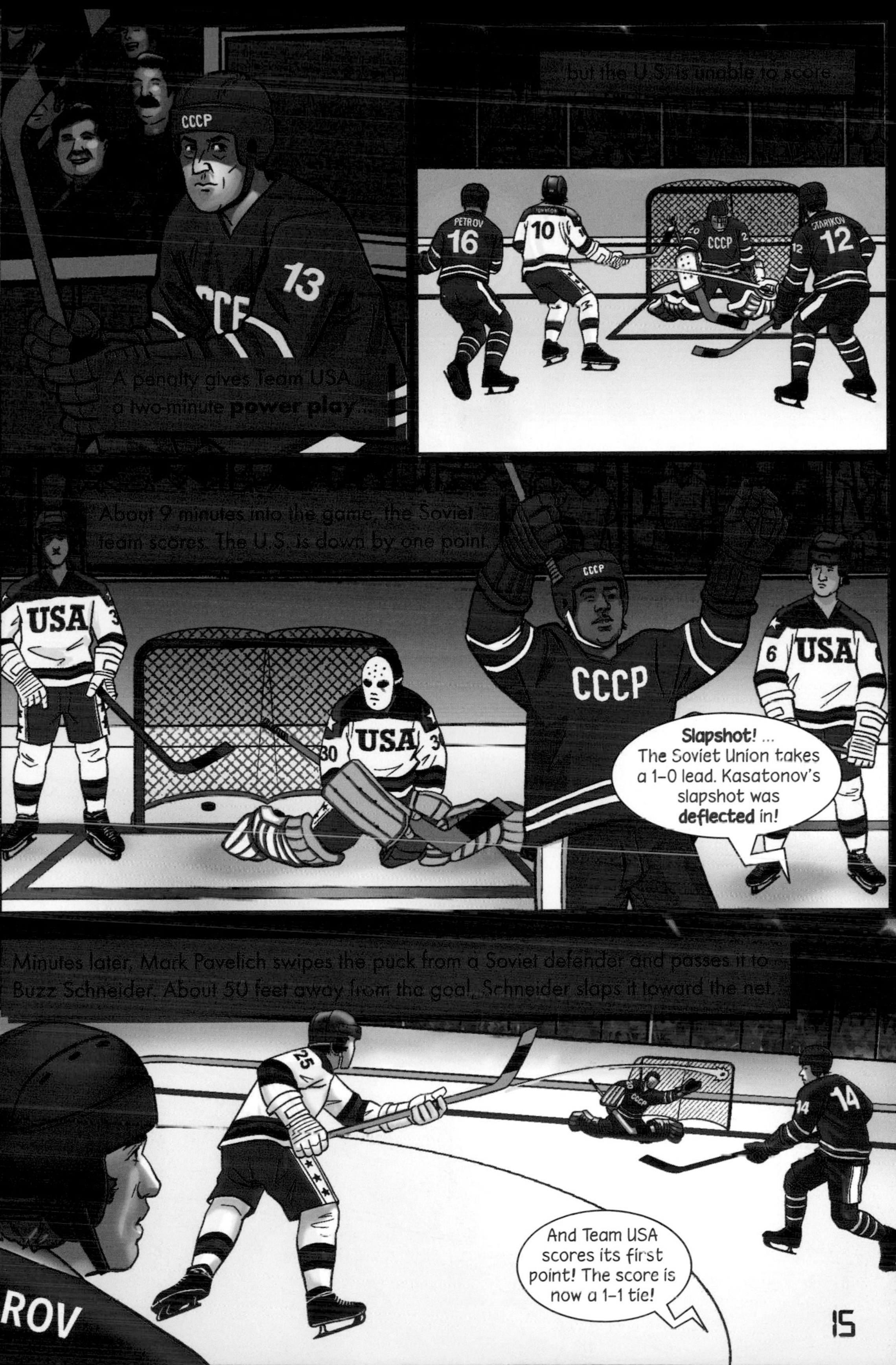
A penalty gives Team USA a two-minute **power play**...
...but the U.S. is unable to score.
About 9 minutes into the game, the Soviet team scores. The U.S. is down by one point.
**Slapshot!** ... The Soviet Union takes a 1–0 lead. Kasatonov's slapshot was **deflected** in!
Minutes later, Mark Pavelich swipes the puck from a Soviet defender and passes it to Buzz Schneider. About 50 feet away from the goal, Schneider slaps it toward the net.
And Team USA scores its first point! The score is now a 1–1 tie!

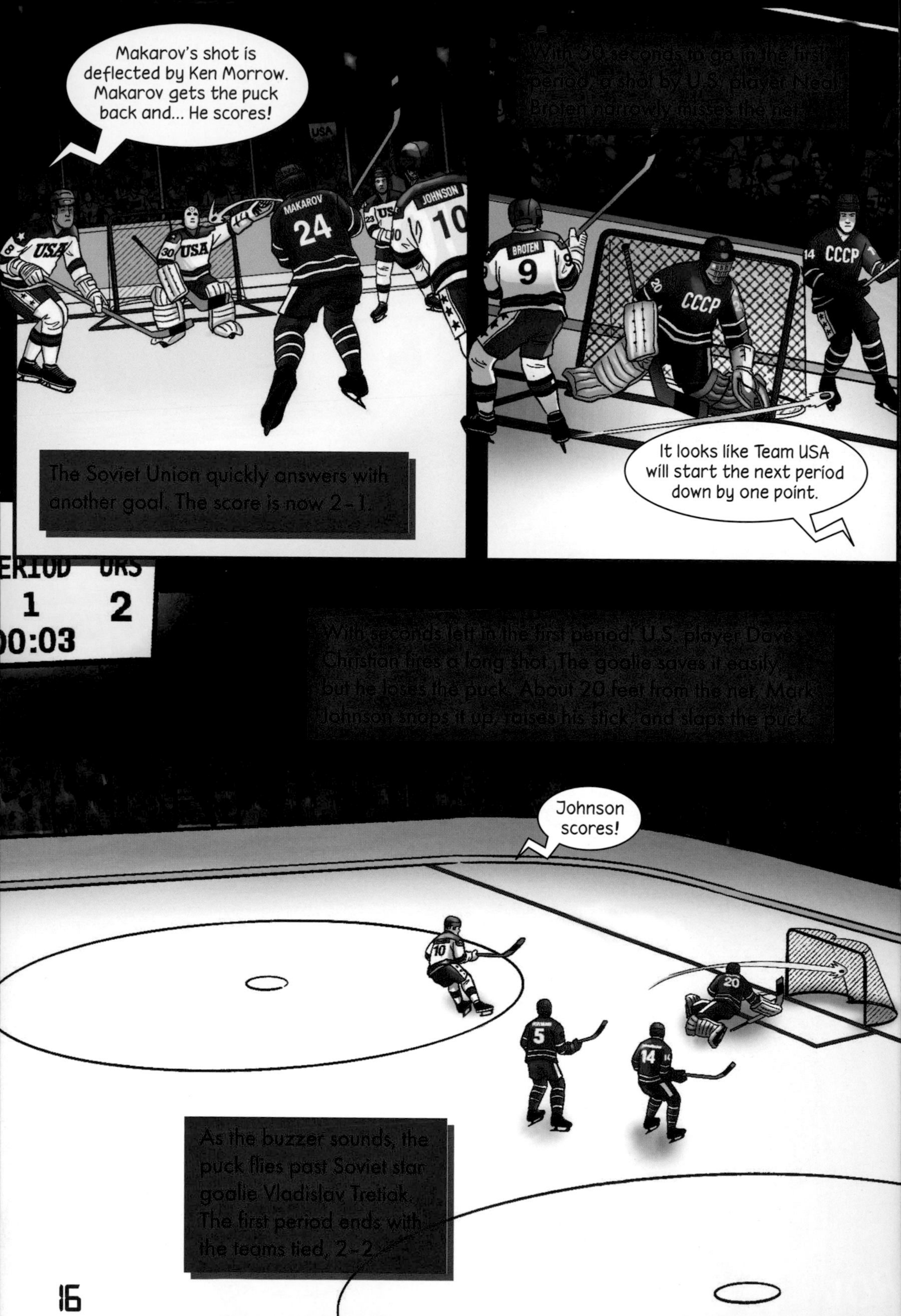
Makarov's shot is deflected by Ken Morrow. Makarov gets the puck back and... He scores!
The Soviet Union quickly answers with another goal. The score is now 2–1.
With 50 seconds to go in the first period, a shot by U.S. player Neal Broten narrowly misses the net.
It looks like Team USA will start the next period down by one point.
With seconds left in the first period, U.S. player Dave Christian fires a long shot. The goalie saves it easily, but he loses the puck. About 20 feet from the net, Mark Johnson snaps it up, raises his stick, and slaps the puck.
Johnson scores!
As the buzzer sounds, the puck flies past Soviet star goalie Vladislav Tretiak. The first period ends with the teams tied, 2–2.

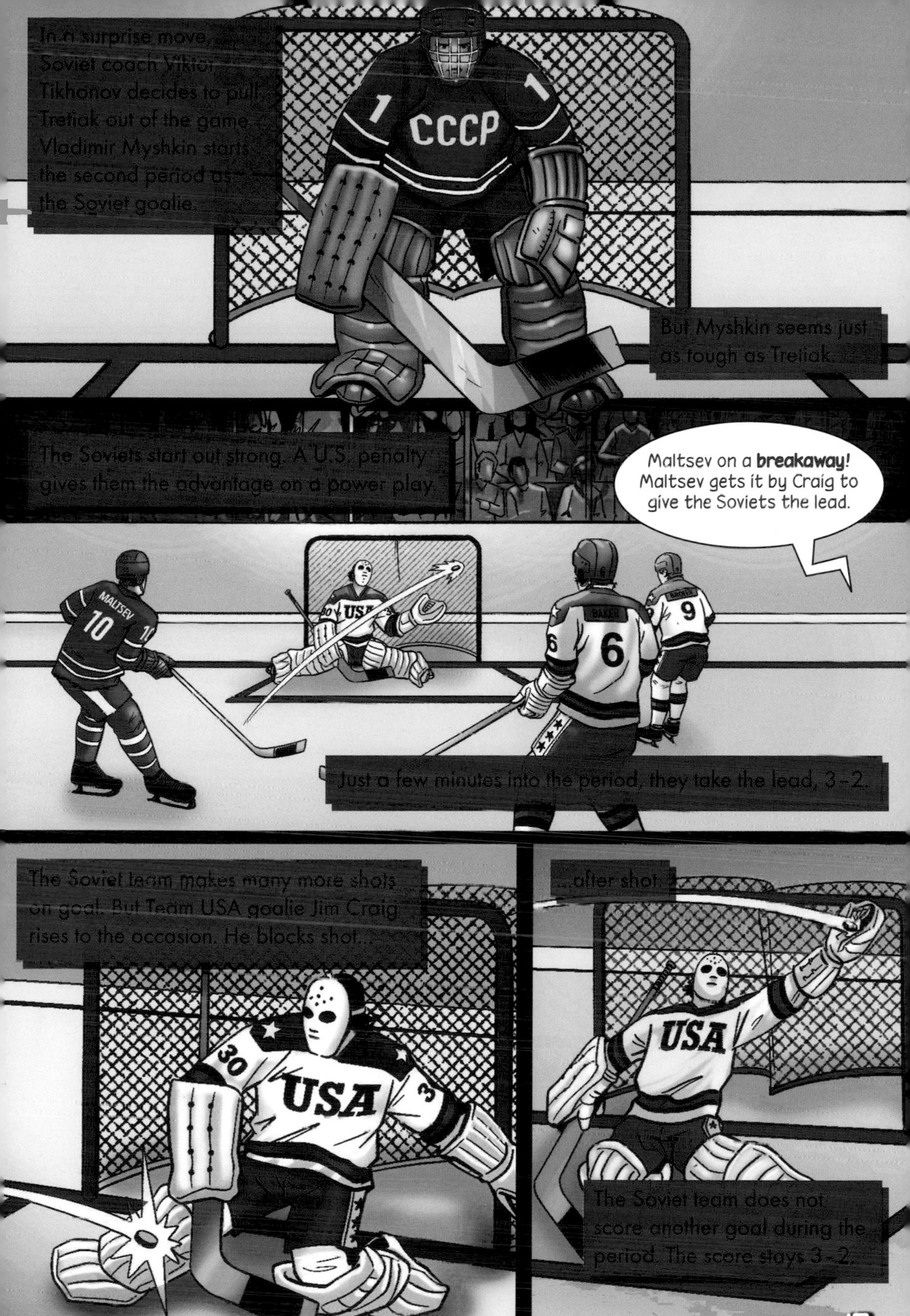
In a surprise move, Soviet coach Viktor Tikhonov decides to pull Tretiak out of the game. Vladimir Myshkin starts the second period as the Soviet goalie.
CCCP
But Myshkin seems just as tough as Tretiak.
The Soviets start out strong. A U.S. penalty gives them the advantage on a power play.
Maltsev on a **breakaway!** Maltsev gets it by Craig to give the Soviets the lead.
MALTSEV
USA
BAKER
Just a few minutes into the period, they take the lead, 3–2.
The Soviet team makes many more shots on goal. But Team USA goalie Jim Craig rises to the occasion. He blocks shot...
...after shot.
USA
USA
The Soviet team does not score another goal during the period. The score stays 3–2.

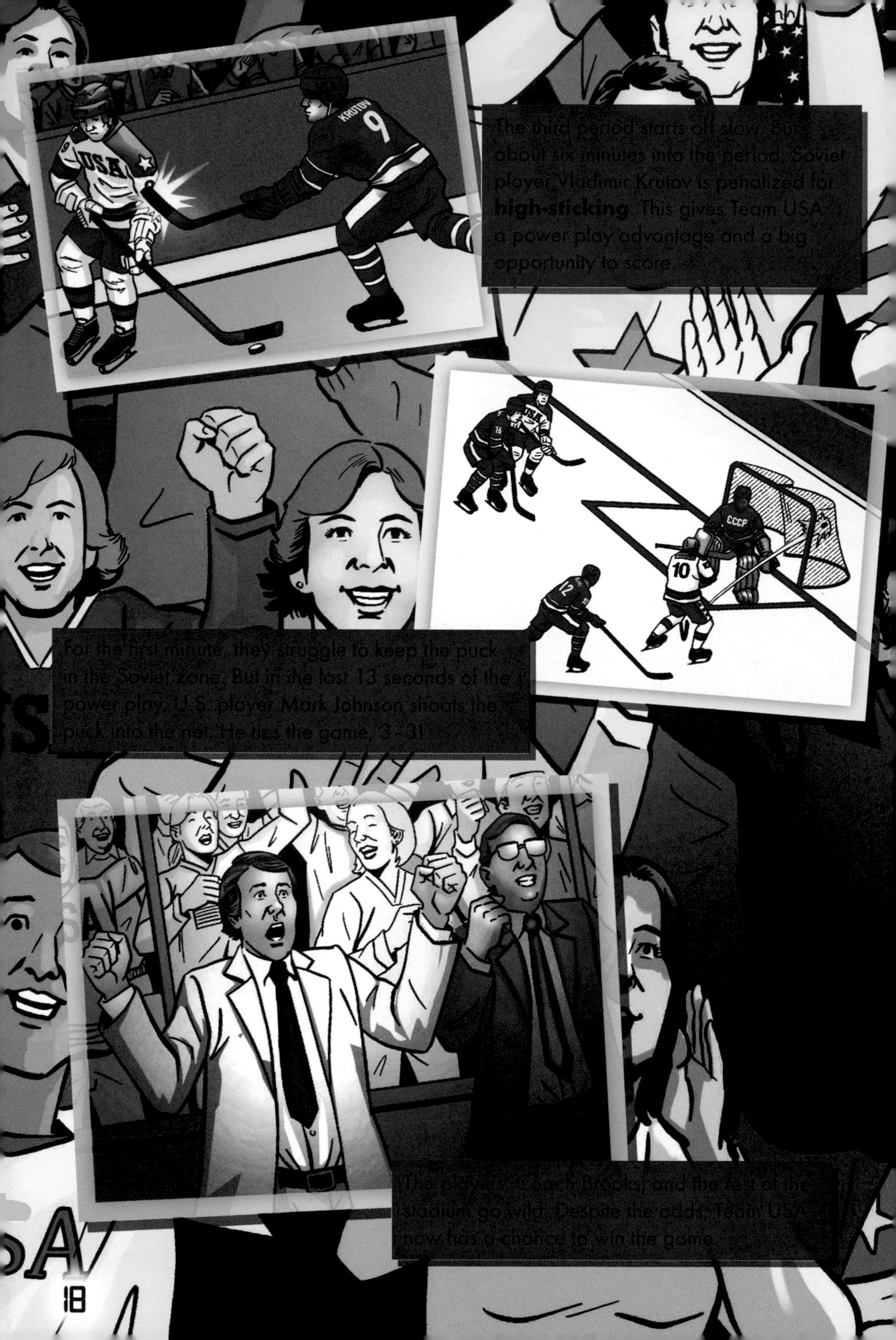
The third period starts off slow. But about six minutes into the period, Soviet player Vladimir Krutov is penalized for **high-sticking**. This gives Team USA a power play advantage and a big opportunity to score.
KRUTOV 9
USA
16
CCCP
10
12
For the first minute, they struggle to keep the puck in the Soviet zone. But in the last 13 seconds of the power play, U.S. player Mark Johnson shoots the puck into the net. He ties the game, 3–3!
The players, Coach Brooks, and the rest of the stadium go wild. Despite the odds, Team USA now has a chance to win the game.

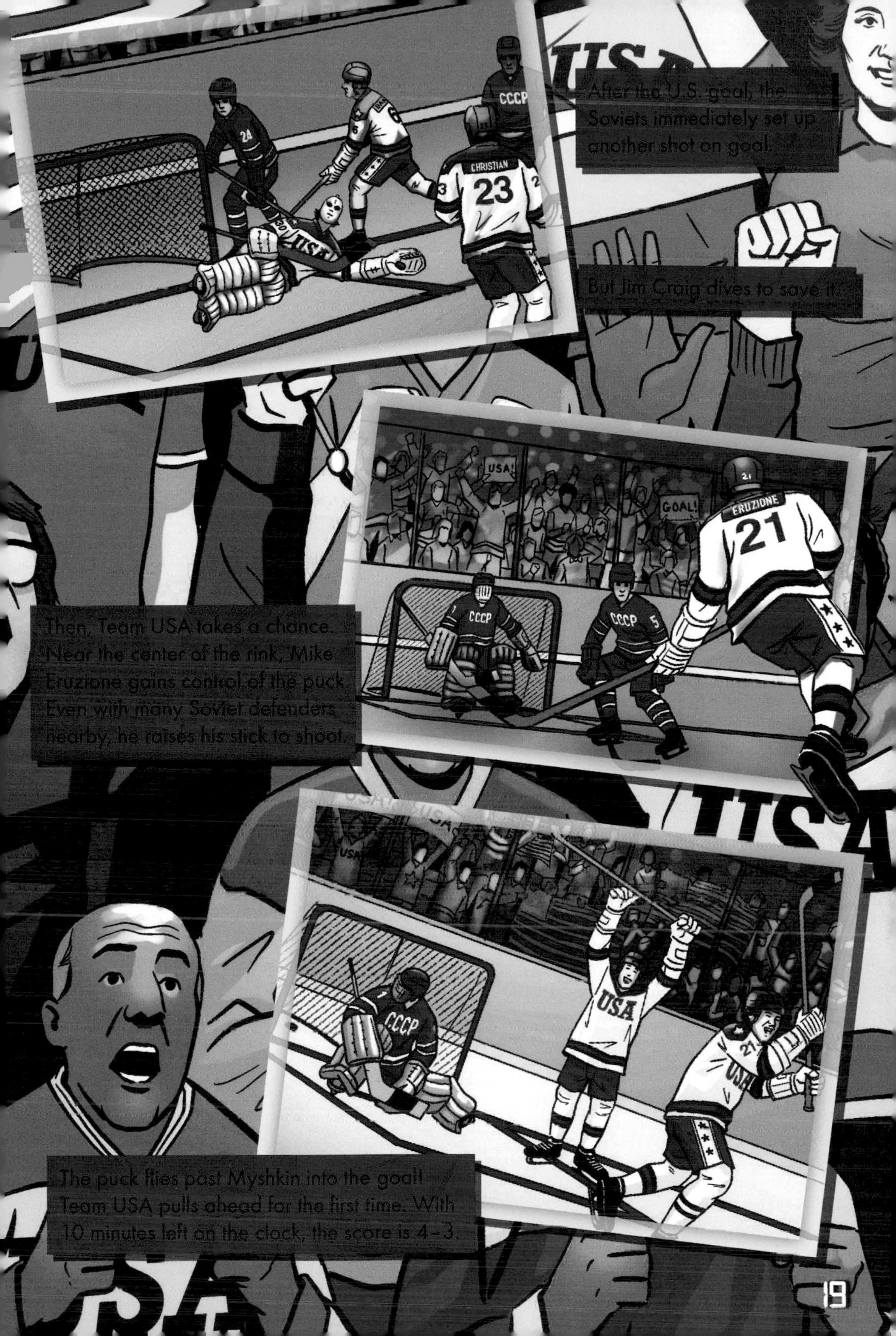
CCCP
CHRISTIAN
23
USA
After the U.S. goal, the Soviets immediately set up another shot on goal.
But Jim Craig dives to save it.
USA!
GOAL!
ERUZIONE
21
CCCP
Then, Team USA takes a chance. Near the center of the rink, Mike Eruzione gains control of the puck. Even with many Soviet defenders nearby, he raises his stick to shoot.
CCCP
USA
The puck flies past Myshkin into the goal! Team USA pulls ahead for the first time. With 10 minutes left on the clock, the score is 4–3.

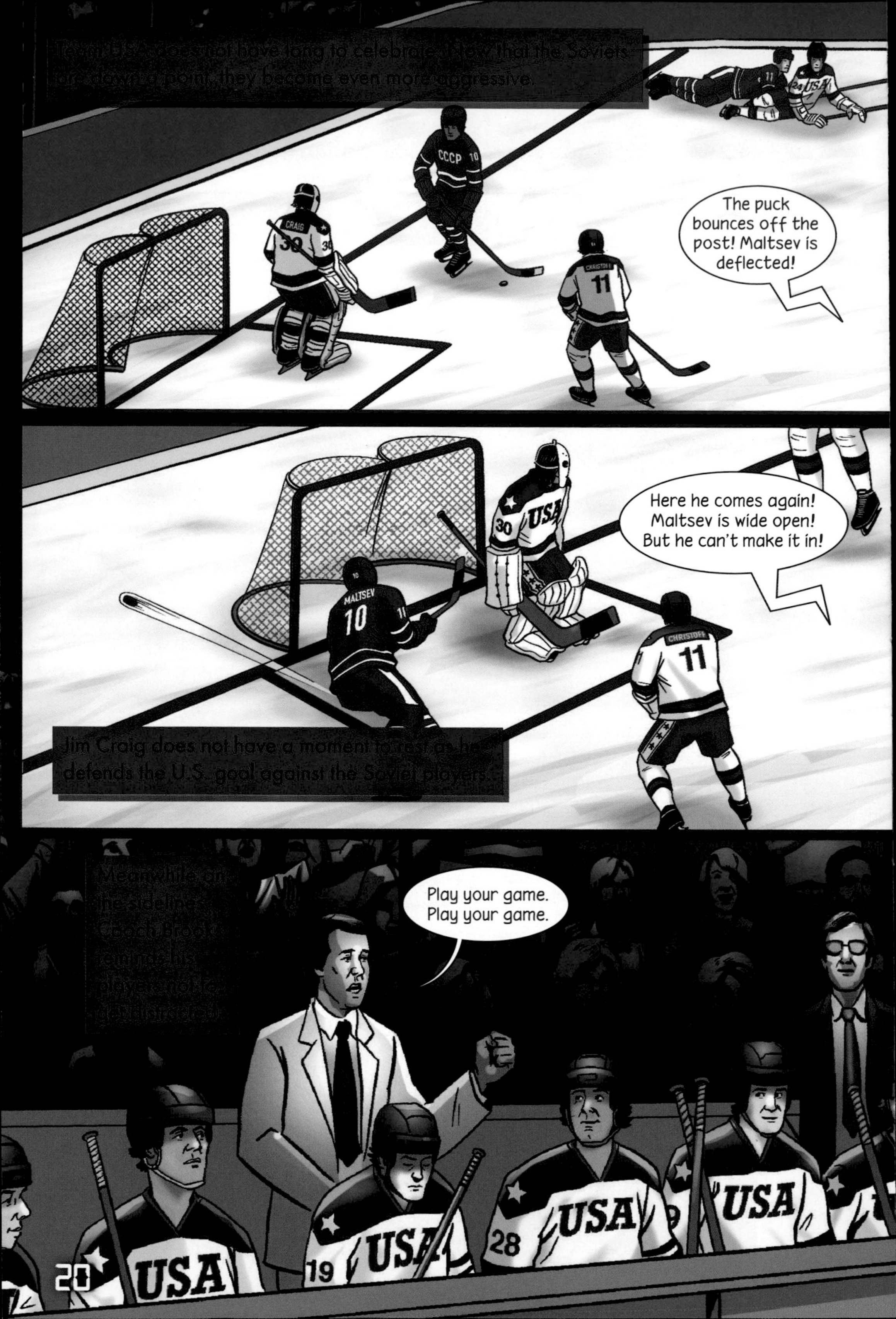
Team USA does not have long to celebrate. Now that the Soviets are down a point, they become even more aggressive.
The puck bounces off the post! Maltsev is deflected!
Here he comes again! Maltsev is wide open! But he can't make it in!
Jim Craig does not have a moment to rest as he defends the U.S. goal against the Soviet players.
Play your game. Play your game.

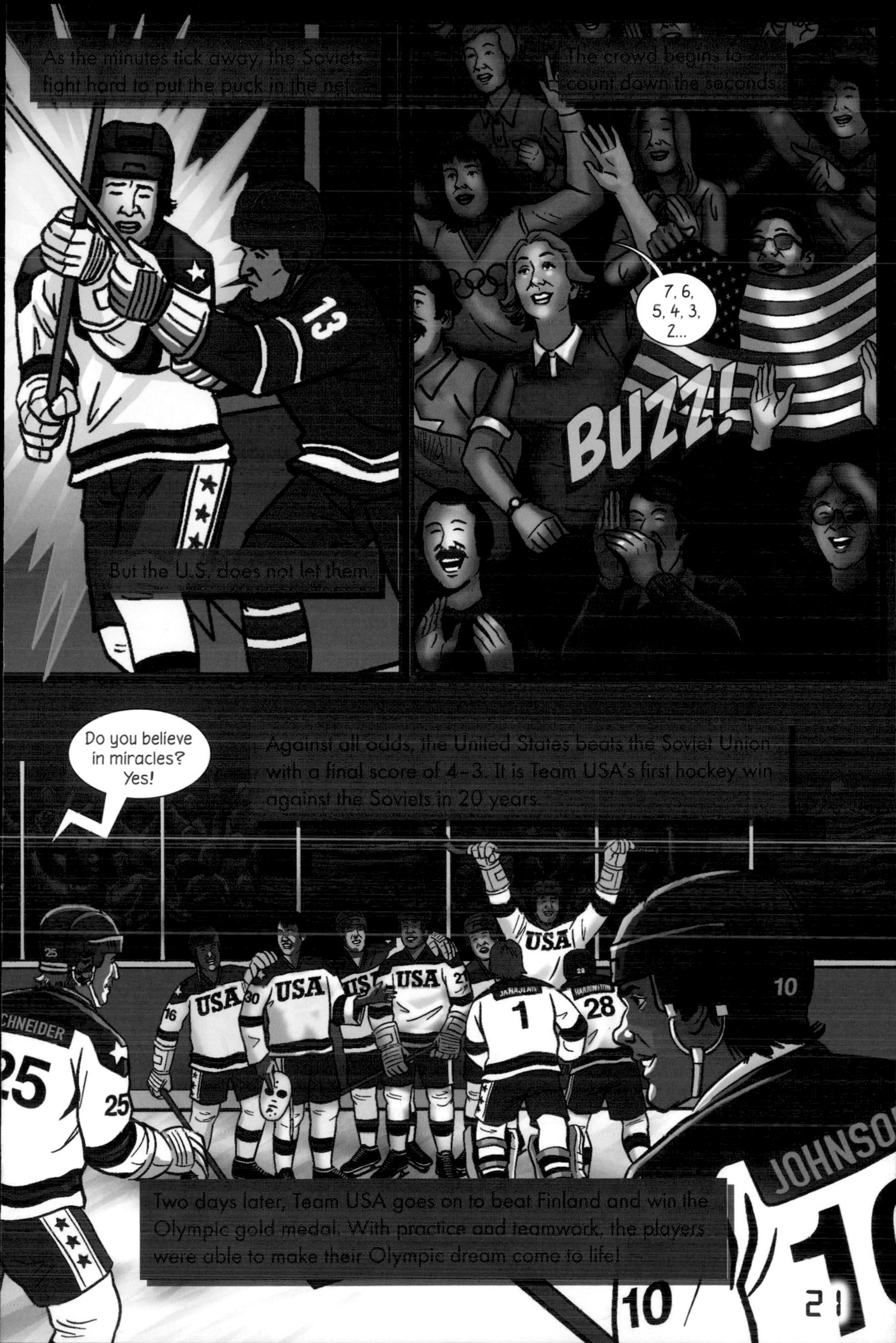
As the minutes tick away, the Soviets fight hard to put the puck in the net.
But the U.S. does not let them.
The crowd begins to count down the seconds.
7, 6, 5, 4, 3, 2...
BUZZ!
Against all odds, the United States beats the Soviet Union with a final score of 4–3. It is Team USA's first hockey win against the Soviets in 20 years.
Do you believe in miracles? Yes!
Two days later, Team USA goes on to beat Finland and win the Olympic gold medal. With practice and teamwork, the players were able to make their Olympic dream come to life!

# MORE ABOUT THE MIRACLE ON ICE

- The 1980 U.S. hockey team was the youngest in national team history. The youngest player was 19, and the oldest was 25.

- The Soviet Union's hockey team went on to win the silver medal at the 1980 Winter Olympics.

- Herb Brooks coached Team USA in the 2002 Winter Olympics. Exactly 22 years after the events of the Miracle on Ice, the U.S. beat Russia once again in the semi-finals.

- In 2004, Disney released *Miracle*, a movie about the 1980 U.S. Olympic hockey team.

# THE MIRACLE ON ICE TIMELINE

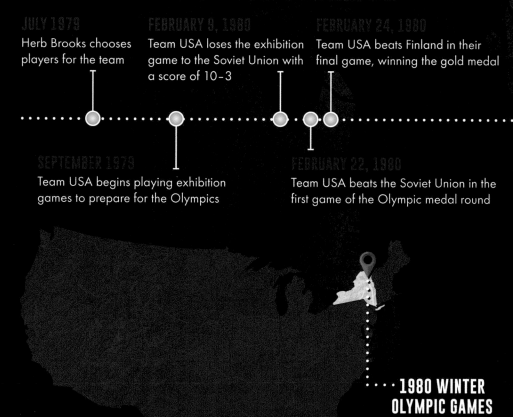

**JULY 1979**
Herb Brooks chooses players for the team

**FEBRUARY 9, 1980**
Team USA loses the exhibition game to the Soviet Union with a score of 10-3

**FEBRUARY 24, 1980**
Team USA beats Finland in their final game, winning the gold medal

**SEPTEMBER 1979**
Team USA begins playing exhibition games to prepare for the Olympics

**FEBRUARY 22, 1980**
Team USA beats the Soviet Union in the first game of the Olympic medal round

**1980 WINTER OLYMPIC GAMES**
**LAKE PLACID, NEW YORK**

# GLOSSARY

aggressive—forceful

bag skates—exercises that involve skating back and forth across the ice at a high speed for a long period of time

breakaway—a time when a player has the puck and there are no defending players between them and the goalie

Cold War—a conflict between the United States and the Soviet Union that lasted from 1945 to 1991

conditioning—training to become a certain way or get used to a certain thing

deflected—forced to change direction

exhibition games—games played to show off a team's skill; exhibition games usually have no impact on a team's rankings.

high-sticking—the act of hitting an opposing player on or above their shoulders with the stick; high-sticking is a penalty in hockey.

medal round—the round of the Olympics during which teams compete for a medal

morale—how a person or group feels about a situation

penalty—a punishment for breaking a rule

power play—an advantage a team receives when the opposing team gets a penalty and must play one player short for a certain amount of time

rival—a long-standing opponent

roster—a list of people on a team

slapshot—a shot made by raising the stick and hitting the puck with a slapping motion

Soviet—related to the Soviet Union; the Soviet Union was a country that spanned across eastern Europe and northern Asia from 1922 to 1991.

tension—a state of unfriendliness

# TO LEARN MORE

## AT THE LIBRARY

Gish, Ashley. *Ice Hockey*. Mankato, Minn.: Creative Education, 2022.

Moening, Kate. *The Cold War*. Minneapolis, Minn.: Bellwether Media, 2024.

Williams, Heather. *Miracle on Ice*. Ann Arbor, Mich.: Cherry Lake Publishing, 2019.

## ON THE WEB

# FACTSURFER

Factsurfer.com gives you a safe, fun way to find more information.

1. Go to www.factsurfer.com
2. Enter "Miracle on Ice" into the search box and click 🔍.
3. Select your book cover to see a list of related content.

# INDEX